Original title:
Life, Laughter, and a Little Confusion

Copyright © 2025 Creative Arts Management OÜ
All rights reserved.

Author: Natalia Harrington
ISBN HARDBACK: 978-1-80566-277-8
ISBN PAPERBACK: 978-1-80566-572-4

## The Jests and Recognitions

In a world where socks may roam,
Missing their mates far from home.
The cat winks with a sly little grin,
As to who really wears the pants, who can win?

A pie falls from the sky, what a treat!
Landed right on a man with two left feet.
He laughs so hard, he can barely stand,
While the dog snickers, a conspirator planned.

The clock strikes twelve; it's time for tea,
But the kettle's dancing, quite carelessly.
It sings a tune, much out of key,
Tune in your favorite, it's a cacophony!

Confetti rains from the light above,
Whispers of magic, a twist of love.
With giggles sprouting from every side,
In the shenanigans, we all take pride.

## The Echo of Joyful Mayhem

A squirrel wearing a tiny hat, you see,
Holds a meeting for all that can't be!
They chatter and scurry, full of glee,
What's on the agenda? A grand picnic spree!

A rooster crows at the break of day,
Wakes up the pig who's fast asleep, hey!
They trade silly stories over coffee mugs,
While dodging the bubbles from waterlogged rugs.

A pair of shoes, mismatched and bright,
Leaps from the closet, ready for flight.
They tap dance across the kitchen floor,
Swirling and twirling, wanting more!

Amidst the chaos, a trumpet sounds,
A parade of laughter, joy abounds.
For in the mess, the heart truly knows,
That the best of days come with wild throws!

## **The Happy Paradox**

A pancake flips, a syrupy flight,
Land on a baby's head, what a sight!
The giggle it starts is a joyful song,
As sticky fingers dance all day long.

A sofa cushions the dreams of the bold,
Where whispers and secrets are ever told.
But beware of the cat, on a mission she's set,
To find out just who is the greatest pet!

Umbrellas swell in the wind's wild play,
A dance party starts on a rainy day.
With puddles as partners and skies upside down,
They twirl and spin in a wiggly town.

In the chaos of cheer, a mess we embrace,
For each crooked smile lights up the place.
From the silly to sweet, in this tangled odd,
We find joy abundant, a blessing from God.

**Swaying in the Accordion of Time**

In a dance with the ticking clock,
Steps are missed, but that's okay.
A twist and a turn, oh what a shock,
We giggle along, come what may.

Each moment a note in the playful tune,
Some flat, some sharp, what a great mess.
We sway to the music, under the moon,
And cherish the chaos, no need to stress.

## Serendipity's Silly Stroll

Stumbled upon a cat in a hat,
It winked and danced across the lane.
A dog in boots joined with a spat,
Together, they made the world a game.

With ice cream dripping and laughter loud,
We twirled past the quirks of the day.
Each mishap feels like a curious crowd,
In the parade of silly, we sway.

## The Riddle of Radiant Days

The sun hides behind a fuzzy cloud,
Yet laughter spills like lemonade.
Puzzles dance, both silly and proud,
In the riddle, confusion won't fade.

A rubber duck floats on a stream,
Waves of wonder, what can it mean?
Whispers of whimsy become the dream,
As chuckles stitch life, bright and clean.

## Frolics Under the Mysterious Moon

Under the glow of a cheeky light,
We chase shadows, bouncing with glee.
A rabbit hops in a mock fight,
Taunting us to join his spree.

Around the trees, we spin and glide,
With giggles echoing through the night.
In folly's embrace, our hearts reside,
Laughter lingers, pure delight.

## Whirlwinds of Whimsy

In a world spun round and round,
Upside down we often found.
Chasing socks that slipped away,
Laughter marks another day.

With pancakes sticking to the wall,
We dance around the morning call.
The cat steals toast, a daring thief,
Creating chaos, bringing grief.

Noses sneezed in unexpected gusts,
Sprinkled giggles turn to rust.
A tumble here, a stumble there,
Life's a circus, take a dare!

So grab a broom and join the ride,
Let's sweep confusion to the side.
With whimsy wrapped around our hearts,
In this chaos, joy imparts.

## The Comedy of Existence

On a stage where shadows play,
Scripts re-written every day.
Fumbles shared, an awkward grin,
The punchline lost, the laughter thin.

With jumbled thoughts and socked feet,
We trip on banter, oh so sweet.
A coffee spill, the room erupts,
In silly moments we interrupt.

A jester's hat, a smile bright,
Turns mundane into pure delight.
The world's a gag, we giggle through,
No need for scripts or perfect cue.

So raise your glass, let's toast to fun,
To moments wild, and all undone.
In this jesters' dance we twirl,
In the comedy, our hearts unfurl.

## **A Tapestry of Amusement**

We weave a tale of uptight threads,
Worn-out sneakers, whispers spread.
A sun hat flies, a dog runs past,
In this madness, joy holds fast.

Juggling tasks, we drop and laugh,
Silly mishaps on our behalf.
A rogue banana, a slip and slide,
In life's playground, we take pride.

From puzzled looks to wily winks,
Each moment drips, a paint that links.
With threads of humor stitched so tight,
We craft a quilt of sheer delight.

So gather round, let's share the cheer,
In silly tales, our hearts draw near.
For in this weave of jest, we find,
A vibrant tie, both sweet and blind.

**The Symphony of the Unconventional**

In a symphony of raucous glee,
Offbeat rhythms set us free.
A clanging pot, a discordant note,
In every laugh, there's joy afloat.

Bouncing balls and slippery floors,
Echoing calls from open doors.
Mismatched socks and tangled souls,
In harmony, the laughter rolls.

Each quirky step, a dance we make,
In swirling joy, the heartstrings shake.
Flipped pancakes fly, a breakfast show,
In this strange act, we freely throw.

So raise your voices, let it ring,
In unconventional, we take wing.
With every chuckle, every cheer,
In this wild song, we draw near.

## Gleeful Gaps and Fillings

In the middle of a happy thought,
A banana slipped, and down I fought.
Chasing giggles along the way,
Tripping over clouds of play.

An umbrella opens in a breeze,
Puddles splash like giggling seas.
With every turn, a new delight,
Chasing shadows in the light.

Lemonade spills on worn-out shoes,
Unexpected mixed colors and hues.
Each little slip, a spark of glee,
Filling up my cup with spree.

A paper hat that wouldn't stay,
Swirling dreams in bright array.
With every laugh, a story spun,
These silly breaks are never done.

## The Curious Collection of Joyful Blunders

A hat too big, a shoe that squeaks,
An unexpected dance, oh, how it peaks!
With every misstep, stories grow,
A gallery of fun in vibrant flow.

Running late with mismatched socks,
Tripping over silly rocks.
A little wink and cheeky grin,
Let the wild troubles begin!

When coffee spills on Monday's best,
It turns into a snicker fest.
Every mishap births a cheer,
A whimsical world we hold dear.

A grand parade of fluffed-up hair,
Funny faces everywhere.
Collecting moments, quirky and sweet,
With giggles, life feels complete.

## **Threads of Amusement**

A stitch gone wrong, what a delight,
Wobbly lines dance in the light.
Crafting joy from bits untold,
Silly secrets woven bold.

The needle slips, a running thread,
Weaving tales from what we said.
Giggling at patterns that don't align,
Every twist, a little divine.

Fuzzy yarn in colors bright,
Makes even the grumpies ignite.
In tangled webs, we find our way,
Chasing chuckles every day.

A patchwork quilt of laughter shared,
Exchanging smiles, none are spared.
With every pull, the seams may fray,
Yet joy is stitched, come what may.

## **A Symphony of Sassy Surprises**

A quirky tune greets the morn,
Blending chaos with a yawn.
Rumbling bellies start to sing,
With unexpected joy they bring.

Wobbling leaders in a conga line,
Footloose and fancy, quite divine.
A dash to the left, a twirl to the right,
Each silly step feels so right.

Bouncing notes like rubber balls,
Grinning friends in empty halls.
An offbeat rhythm takes the stage,
With every blunder, we engage.

A crashing cymbal, a tuba's cheer,
Unexpected echoes that we hear.
In harmony with silly sounds,
A merry heart as laughter bounds.

## **Mischief Beneath the Sun**

Bubbles burst in fleeting air,
Chasing giggles everywhere.
Puppies dance on frolic's stage,
Winks exchanged, we turn the page.

Silly hats and mismatched socks,
Juggling dreams like old wood blocks.
Lemonade spills, oh what a scene,
Sun kissed cheeks, and laughter's sheen.

Foot races end in tumble and fall,
Squeaky toys and playful brawl.
With every hop, a new surprise,
In this world, we improvise.

So here's to jesters in the day,
Crafting smiles in their own way.
With twinkling eyes, the heart runs wild,
Mischief thrives in every child.

## Joyful Jumbles

Jigsaw pieces all askew,
Lost a shoe, found a clue.
Rainboots dance in puddle throng,
Twisted tales where we belong.

Whimsical whispers, stories blend,
Pancakes flip, and syrup sends.
Cereal spills in morning's light,
Fruit loops twirl, a rainbow fight.

Laughter rings in sweetest tunes,
Upside down beneath the moons.
Chasing thoughts as they collide,
With silly jokes, we let them slide.

Grinning wide, the heart's delight,
In this chaos, we ignite.
Mix and mingle, join the fun,
Every moment's just begun.

## **Chasing Shadows and Sunshine**

Candles flicker, shadows dance,
Frantic steps in merry prance.
Chasing echoes of our glee,
Hiding behind the old oak tree.

Silly whispers through the breeze,
Tickling noses, oh, such tease.
Sunglasses on, we strut around,
With each smile, the joy is found.

Playful pranks and clever charms,
Open arms and wide-eyed balms.
Every twist brings laughter loud,
We weave our dreams within the crowd.

So here we glide on sunlit paths,
Counting giggles, feeling laughs.
In this chase, we'll find our way,
Shadows blend with bright today.

## The Enigma of Everyday Smiles

Polka dots on left and right,
Bizarre hats, a funny sight.
Chasing tales with cups of tea,
Puzzle pieces of what could be.

Socks that match? A distant theme,
Bubble wrap and ice cream dreams.
Balloons whisper secrets stored,
As silly antics can't be ignored.

Through ups and downs, we find the spark,
Lighthearted glances in the park.
What's the riddle? What's the game?
Each twist of joy keeps us the same.

So let us ponder, giggle, play,
In this riddle of our day.
Confusion turns to playful styles,
Unraveling with everyday smiles.

## Echoes of Joyful Whimsy

A squirrel stole my sandwich,
With nimble little paws,
I chased him round the park,
But he paused for applause.

The birds giggled in the trees,
As I tumbled on the grass,
They must have found it funny,
Watching me alas.

A busker played a tune,
That made the pigeons dance,
While I just stood in awe,
Dreaming of my chance.

So here's to silly moments,
And the joy that they bring,
In a world that spins around,
Let's laugh and dance and sing.

## The Dance of Everyday Oddities

A cat in a bowtie, fancy tricks,
Waltzed right past my shopping cart,
It seemed the world was upside down,
Confusion played the part.

My coffee jumped from the table,
In a splash of milky cheer,
I questioned all my choices,
As it vanished in mid-air.

Umbrellas turned into kites,
As the wind began to roar,
I just held on tightly,
As I drifted 'cross the floor.

So let's embrace the quirky,
With giggles in each glance,
In this dance of oddities,
Join me for a chance.

## Serenade of Serendipity

I found a mismatched sock,
Dancing on the lawn,
It led a merry jig,
Until the dawn was gone.

A dog with shoes on backwards,
Chased after its own tail,
While I just stood there laughing,
In a whimsical detail.

A man in a tutu grinned,
While jogging near the park,
His cheerful spirit glowed,
Even when it got dark.

Surprises bloom around us,
In the silliest of ways,
Let's sing this serenade,
For odd and joyful days.

## Chuckles in the Chaos

A blender went on strike,
Amidst the morning rush,
As I stood in confusion,
With a tomato in a hush.

My phone decided to sing,
A tune from yesterday,
I danced without a reason,
And laughed the day away.

The cat knocked over papers,
In a feat of high finesse,
But who could blame that feline,
It was all just a jest.

So here's to strange adventures,
And the giggles that they bring,
In this chaos we find comfort,
And joy in everything.

## Echoes of a Chuckling Breeze

In a park where the birdies sing,
Squirrels dance, chasing their bling.
The sun winks with a cheeky glow,
Clouds giggle as they drift slow.

A jolly breeze whispers secret tales,
Of tangled shoes and floppy sails.
Laughter bounces, flips, and spins,
Tickles the trees, and hugs your skin.

Shadows stretch and play hide and seek,
While daisies nod, their joy unique.
Puddles splash with a sudden cheer,
Reflecting goofy grins so near.

As day bows down, the sky turns pink,
The world grins wide, don't you think?
Echoes of joy, a constant tease,
In a park where the birdies sneeze.

## **Tangles of Tickle and Thought**

A curious cat with a curious plan,
Decides to dance like a silly man.
With a twist and a turn, it gives a whirl,
Sending papers flying; oh, what a swirl!

The clock ticks slow in a wobbly way,
While socks plot mischief for another day.
A teacup giggles, spills a bit,
As cookies type scripts, never to quit.

In sweet chaos, a cake takes flight,
Landing on heads, oh what a sight!
Butterflies yum on laughter-laced breeze,
Chasing the tickles that dance with ease.

Oh, the joy of a topsy-turvy thought,
Where all the goofiness is perfectly caught.
In a world of wonder, we twirl and toss,
Finding sheer glee in the minor loss.

## The Mirthful Maze


Inside a maze of mirth and jest,
Hats spin around like they're on a quest.
Trees wear glasses, quite out of style,
While flowers chuckle with a cheeky smile.

A dog in a bowtie offers you cheer,
Jumps over puddles, a champion here.
Balloons float by with a snicker so bold,
Whispering secrets that never get old.

The sun's in a tangle, a flare of red,
Getting tested by thoughts in its head.
The paths are zigzagged, filled with glee,
As laughter echoes, setting us free.

Chasing the giggles around every bend,
In this maze of cheer, there's never an end.
Winding through chuckles with grace untold,
Finding sweet treasures of humor and gold.

## Dancing on a Tightrope of Joy

Above the ground, with a skip and a hop,
A jester giggles, refusing to stop.
Balancing dreams on a flip-floppy line,
Catching the sparkle of stars that shine.

Wobbly dancers on clouds made of cream,
Sipping on laughter, living the dream.
An owl claps, with a wink and a flare,
As the moon snorts—oh, what a pair!

Whirling around with a kick and a spin,
Finding bright chuckles tucked deep within.
The rope sings songs of absurd delight,
As magic unfolds under soft, silver light.

With each teeter, joy beckons anew,
On this tightrope, there's room for you too.
Embrace the giggles, let troubles float,
For joy is the circus, a merry old coat.

## Serenade of the Silliness

A cat in a hat sings a tune,
While dancing with socks by the light of the moon.
Chickens play chess in the backyard,
It's quite an odd sight, I must say, not marred.

Lemonade rivers flow down the street,
Where gumdrops and laughter together do meet.
Silly hats worn by all who roam,
Each step is a giggle, a tickle of home.

## The Art of Delightful Chaos

Marbles roll wild on a banana peel,
A waltz with the toaster, oh what a reel!
Jellybeans tumble from pockets so deep,
As grandmas on skateboards take leaps that leap.

Cupcakes are flying, what a great sight,
With sprinkles that twinkle in the soft light.
Mismatched socks giggle as they parade,
In this dance of the daft, the serious, we trade.

## Riddles Laced with Grins

What has four wheels and flies on the wall?
A garbage truck, with a very loud call.
Bananas in pajamas stroll down the lane,
Spilling confetti and jiggling in rain.

Why did the tomato turn red, you inquire?
It saw the salad dressing, and couldn't help fire.
Noodles on bicycles ride into the sun,
Around every corner, the laughter's begun.

## Wandering Through Whims

A frog in a bowtie invites you to dance,
While cookies do cartwheels in a playful trance.
Clouds made of candy float high above,
As a whirlwind of giggles surrounds us with love.

Hats that are talking insist on a joke,
While trees spread their branches as if they can poke.
In this waltz of whimsy, we twirl and we spin,
With shadows of silliness wrapped like a grin.

## Giggles Beneath the Surface

In a world that spins and sways,
A cat in socks begins to play.
Chasing tails and silly dreams,
Hiding under beds, or so it seems.

With cupcakes flying through the air,
A dance-off with a garden chair.
A squirrel chases its own tail,
While giggles echo, never pale.

A rubber chicken tells a joke,
And suddenly the room's awoke.
Bright balloons float high and free,
As smiles bloom like flowers, you see!

Underneath the silver stars,
We find humor in our scars.
Embracing chaos, having fun,
With every laugh, we become one.

## Mirth in the Midst of Mayhem

When spoons become a drum brigade,
And laughter spills, a joyous cascade.
Cakes that wobble, mischief abound,
In every corner, glee is found.

Socks on hands and hats askew,
A playful prank, who knew it grew?
With jelly sprawled across the floor,
A silly dance, we want more.

An octopus in a chef's hat,
Whisking pancakes, imagine that!
As giggles bounce like bouncing beans,
Through chaotic scenes on movie screens.

Confetti rains from scattered skies,
With every laugh, a sweet surprise.
In this whirlwind, kind of mad,
A hint of wild makes us glad.

## A Carousel of Curious Moments

Round and round, the merry-go,
A penguin in a bright red bow.
With unicorns and cake on top,
We spin and twirl, we never stop.

A jester juggles apples high,
As squirrels laugh and start to fly.
The wind whispers silly haikus,
To every child who dares to choose.

In puddles deep, reflections gleam,
Where silly shadows form a dream.
A rubber duck in a top hat,
Yes, that's where we're really at!

Each twist and turn, a giggle waits,
Surprises hide behind big gates.
Curious moments spin and sway,
As we hop on the crazy train today.

## Laughter's Light on a Twisted Path

Through tangled woods where giggles roam,
We wander far from our safe home.
With owls wearing glasses, wise and bright,
They tell us jokes in the pale moonlight.

A woeful frog sings out a tune,
While fireflies dance, a glowing boon.
We wander on this wobbly track,
With whimsical friends who've got our back.

In puddles deep, we leap and splash,
Amidst the chaos, we may clash.
But laughter bubbles like a stream,
In every twist, a funny theme.

So let us trip and stumble through,
The merry path that's bright and new.
With every laugh, we steer our fate,
On windy roads where joys await.

## The Happy Hiccups of Existence

In the morning, socks don't match,
Coffee spills in a happy patch.
A cat jumps high, lands on my face,
I laugh aloud in this silly space.

The toast pops up, a buttered scare,
I trip on air, no one does care.
A wiggle, a giggle, the world spins round,
Joy found in chaos, the best kind abound.

Friends drop by with wild ideas,
Wearing mismatched shoes and big ol' cheers.
We dance to tunes that are out of key,
Finding the rhythm in absurdity.

So raise a glass to the humorous strife,
Embrace the quirks, it's a comical life.
In every fumble, in every blunder,
Hiccups of joy, like playful thunder.

## Confounding Delight

A penguin waddles down the street,
In search of ice cream, a tasty treat.
A joke gone wrong, it starts a craze,
Who knew such silliness would amaze?

The clocks are melting, time's a prank,
My socks are wet, I spilled my drink!
A dog wears glasses, looks quite bright,
He barks at shadows in pure delight.

I pull on a door marked 'push',
A squirrel giggles, stealing my lunch.
Nonsense reigns in this charming spree,
Confounding glee, just you and me.

So let's embrace the silly chase,
For smiles bloom in the silliest place.
Mirth is found in unexpected ways,
In this merry muddle, joy always stays.

## Tangles of Grins and Gaffes

A hat on my head, three sizes too big,
I dance with a broom, feeling quite sprig.
Spaghetti slips down, a noodle race,
Giggling so hard, can't find my face.

A tickle from shadows, who could it be?
A squirrel named Benny decides to play free.
With laughter in heaps like snow in the air,
We tumble and roll without a care.

An umbrella opens with a pop and a twirl,
I'm soaked in the rain, what a daring whirl!
My shoes are all squeaky, a symphony bright,
In this tangled mess, how perfect the night.

So here's to missteps, let joy take the lead,
In every mishap, there's laughter indeed.
Life's swirls of folly, in comical spins,
With grins and gaffes, the fun truly wins.

## The Joyous Jumble of Being

A sock on my hand, it's a puppet show,
A rubber duck floats, whispers hello.
Chasing the echoes of a wild old spin,
There's laughter and joy tucked right within.

Bad puns collide like a bubble of cheer,
The more they miss, the louder we cheer.
A dance in the kitchen, a raucous affair,
Mixing the groceries with flair and care.

The sun hides behind a cloud for a game,
Then peeks out to see if we're still the same.
With every hiccup, each bizarre delight,
We find together, the world feels just right.

So join me in this jumble of fun,
Where silliness reigns, and we weigh a ton.
In twists and turns, smiles spring out like springs,
In this joyous mess, the heart truly sings.

## **Surprises Wrapped in Smiles**

A frog in a top hat, what a sight,
Dancing under stars that twinkle bright.
As squirrels debate the best nut to eat,
Each giggle unravels at their tiny feet.

A cat with a monocle chases a bee,
Wearing a grin as wide as the sea.
In this world of whimsy, nothing feels wrong,
As joy echoes loud in a silly song.

**Riddles in the Morning Light**

Sun shines on pancakes stacked quite high,
While toast makes a face, a silly goodbye.
Jellybeans jump, first to the floor,
Declaring their victory, wanting more.

Cereal sings from a bright blue bowl,
With a wink and a twist, it takes a stroll.
As laughter breaks forth through flour-dusted air,
Morning's puzzle unfolds, with quirks to spare.

## Glee Amidst the Unraveled

Wooly sweaters dance in a playful breeze,
As mismatched socks declare, "Do as you please!"
A tumble of giggles spills from a drawer,
Where silly socks plot to make us adore.

In the garden, tomatoes wear funny hats,
While daffodils gossip with old alley cats.
Underneath all this joy, there's a twist in the tale,
A riddle wrapped tightly, but never will fail.

## **Mischief on a Paradoxical Path**

A winding path leads to nowhere at all,
While rabbits play parlor, having a ball.
With teacups and saucers, they toast to the moon,
As a clock strikes thirteen—oh, what a tune!

Balloons float by, with secrets they bear,
Whispering tales that tickle the air.
In this realm of oddities, smiles never fade,
For every turn taken, a new game is played.

## Euphoria in Unexpected Places

In the garden of socks, old and mismatched,
A moment of giggles with each step I catch.
The cat in a sunbeam, a queen on her throne,
Chasing her shadow, as if it were bone.

Under the table, the crumbs start to dance,
As a toddler's giggle ignites my glance.
The toast that pops up like a prankster's delight,
Confetti of breakfast, oh what a sight!

A stumble at humor, then straightening up,
With laughter the weight of the world feels less tough.
Forgotten the worries, the chaotic days,
In silly little tidbits, joy softly plays.

For smiles can be found in the oddest of nooks,
In fabric of moments, much better than books.
So here's to the joys that catch us off guard,
In unexpected places, the heart stays unmarred.

## The Jigsaw of Myriad Moments

In a puzzling chatter, the clock's ticking slow,
I fumble with pieces, where does this one go?
A patch from the past with a laugh as it clicks,
Like finding a penny stuck deep in the mix.

Socks populate corners, they dance and they twirl,
Each one a story, each color a whirl.
An umbrella turned inside out at the park,
Shows the sky's humor—a whimsical lark.

The toast falls buttered, like wishes unplanned,
A tale of mischief escapes from my hand.
The wild flowers giggle, ye olde dandelion,
As children play tag with the breeze—ever tryin'.

With crumbs on my shirt and a sock on my foot,
I weave through the chaos, my brain in a hoot.
For moments are puzzles, each piece a delight,
In the jigsaw of days, let the laughter ignite!

## **Echoing Hilarity**

In whispers of giggles, the echoes remain,
Where pranks meet the serious, tickling the brain.
A pancake that flips with a laugh in the air,
Turns breakfast to circus, a flurry to share.

A cat in pajamas sprawls out on the floor,
All legs in a frenzy, a wild little roar.
The dog in a bowtie, he struts with such pride,
Dancing to rhythms that bounce from inside.

The kids play a game, it's called, 'Who's the Boss?'
Messy hairdos, oh dear, someone's at loss.
As they scheme and they plot, with giggles and grins,
An orchestra's worth of their mayhem begins.

So let's walk the tightrope, wonky and free,
Where echoes of humor bring joy, can't you see?
In the chaos of echoes lies laughter untamed,
A melody's heartbeat, forever unframed.

## The Intrigue of Bright Eyed Curiosity

With wide eyes of wonder, the world is anew,
Mysteries hiding in each drop of dew.
A squirrel's acrobatics, a giggle of chance,
In the whirlwind of joy, all the heartstrings dance.

What's inside this box? Is it gold or a shoe?
The quest for an answer, an adventure to brew.
In stories long woven, the plot twists and spins,
Each question a riddle that playfully grins.

A rainbow appears in the mess of my week,
As colors collide, bringing smiles with a peek.
The laughter of children, like bubbles afloat,
In the quest for the quirky, they happily gloat.

So here's to the moments that sparkle and shine,
And curious glances that tickle the spine.
For in the warm chaos of bright-eyed delight,
The intrigue of wonder sets the world alight.

## Twists on the Road to Nowhere

With every turn, a smiling face,
Chasing shadows in a wild maze.
A map that's lost, a giggle or two,
We wander onward, just me and you.

Each pothole's dip, a chance to play,
With every bump, we laugh away.
The signs are crooked, the path unclear,
Yet with your smile, there's naught to fear.

A rainbow shows up with clouds in tow,
Giggle and spin as the winds do blow.
We stumble, we dance, as we spin around,
In this twisted road, joy's always found.

## The Jester's Whirlwind

A hat adorned with quirky charms,
The jester prances, full of alarms.
He trips on purpose, a fall so grand,
With silly antics, we clap our hands.

His jokes are jumbles, a riddle spree,
Each punchline wrapped in mystery.
We laugh 'til sore, our cheeks are red,
A whirlwind of giggles, the heart is fed.

The crowd's a chorus, a playful bunch,
In the chaos, we savor our lunch.
With each performance, the world's a play,
A jester's jest leads us through the day.

## Embracing the Unscripted

The script forgot where it should lead,
Yet spontaneity plants the seed.
With mismatched socks on a sunny morn,
We embrace the chaos, from which we're born.

A spilled drink and a crazy dance,
In the unscripted, we find our chance.
To turn missteps into a fun spree,
With each twist and shout, we feel so free.

The clock is ticking, but we're in pause,
Who needs plans when we've got applause?
Life's a canvas, a curious blend,
In the strokes of jest, we're on the mend.

## Whims of a Wondrous Journey

A suitcase full of dreams and laughs,
We dance through moments, like little drafts.
A flip-flop here and a jump to there,
In every heartbeat, a giggle to share.

The roads are bumpy, the skies may frown,
But joys are scattered all around.
With every wrong turn, a story to weave,
In this wondrous trip, we dare to believe.

Every sunset paints a brand new muse,
In the twilight glow, we cannot lose.
Whims spill over, like confetti in air,
On this journey of wonders, joy is our flare.

## Whirlwinds of Amusement

In a circus of quirks, we spin round,
Chasing giggles that bubble unbound.
A tumble of thoughts, a dance of delight,
Twisted and tangled, we laugh through the night.

The clock tickles time as it winks with a grin,
While parrots squawk tales of where we have been.
We juggle the jests that keep us all bright,
In a whirlwind of wonder, all feels just right.

From upside-down pancakes to shoes on our heads,
We trip over mishaps that fill us with threads.
Each moment a memory, a jest never dull,
In the carnival chaos, our hearts are quite full.

So leap with abandon, take chances galore,
For fun is the key that unlocks every door.
With smiles on our faces, let joy take its flight,
In this whirlwind of giggles, we'll chase the moonlight.

## The Jigsaw Puzzle of Joy

With pieces all scattered, we search high and low,
Pondering puzzles that twist and that flow.
A corner of laughter, a middle of cheer,
We fit in the moments that bring us all near.

Each bit tells a story, some silly, some grand,
As we dance through the chaos, hand in hand.
Turning misfits to miracles in every lost clump,
Magic awakens from every small jump.

Like socks in the dryer, our paths intertwine,
Finding joy in the mix, we've mastered the line.
Tangled with giggles, can't find our own way,
But smiles and mishaps guide us through the play.

So gather the pieces, give laughter a try,
For in every odd corner, our spirits can fly.
In the curious chaos, so colorful, bright,
The jigsaw of moments makes everything right.

## Reveling in Randomness

Dancing with socks that are mismatched and wild,
We stumble and trip, like a clumsy child.
With ice cream splashes and sprinkles on cake,
In this joyful confusion, we're learning to shake.

The randomness reigns, like a game of charades,
As bananas wear hats in the grandest parades.
In a garden of giggles where nonsense blooms free,
We cherish the moments that dare us to be.

Chasing bouncing balloons through a carnival scene,
With laughter like popcorn, both fizzy and keen.
We float on our whims, and no rules hold us back,
As silly surprises fill in every small crack.

So let's revel together in this wacky ballet,
With whimsy as our compass, we'll never lose sway.
For the treasure of joy in the odd and absurd,
Is found in the echoes of fun that we've heard.

## **Flashes of Fun in the Uncertain**

In the flicker of moments, we glance and we grin,
As chuckles and wiggles invite us to spin.
An umbrella that flips in a bluster of wind,
Is just one of the charms that this chaos can send.

With capers and capes, we disguise as we dare,
Hopping through puddles with laughter to spare.
Navigating the flukes of this zany parade,
We find joy in the twists that the universe made.

A toast to the gaffes, to the slips and the falls,
For each unexpected turn brings us giggling calls.
We paint our adventures in hues all our own,
In flashes of whimsy, together we've grown.

So let's dance on the edge of uncertainty bright,
With jokes that ignite and a sparkle of light.
In this playful existence, we find what's bestowed,
In flashes of fun, we embrace the unknown.

## Quirky Chronicles

In a town where socks go missing,
The fridge hums a tune in glee,
Cats wear hats made from wishing,
While teacups dance with glee.

Jellybeans bounce down the street,
Chasing pigeons who don't care,
Umbrellas upside down look neat,
Spinning tales in mid-air.

Bananas break into a jam,
As the clock strikes out of tune,
Chickens form a little band,
To serenade the afternoon.

With every twist and silly joke,
A grin unfolds like spring's bloom,
In the heart of the whimsical folk,
Where confusion paints every room.

## Sips of Sweet Surrealism

A teapot brewed from starlit dreams,
Serves sugar clouds and lemon beams,
Time wobbles like a jellybean,
In a world that feels like a scene.

Marshmallow clouds float in the sky,
While chocolate rivers start to flow,
And whispers of whimsy gently sigh,
As giggles take center stage in the show.

Fish wear goggles; frogs in tuxedos,
Dance their waltz on a beam of light,
With every step, reality slows,
And in this realm, all feels just right.

So take a sip from this surreal cup,
Let the sweetness fill your soul,
As ordinary turns topsy-turns up,
And laughter becomes the ultimate goal.

## Kaleidoscope of Giggles

A rainbow slides down the slide,
Puppies jump in bubbles of cheer,
Each tick of the clock's drumming pride,
Brings moments to dance and jeer.

Funny hats on people parade,
While stars twinkle with a loud roar,
As the sun in a tutu played,
La la la, forevermore.

The trees tell tales of jolly cheer,
While squirrels with monocles sip tea,
With every tickle that we hear,
The whispers of joy blend with glee.

Crayons sketch a world askew,
Where giggles paint the sky so bright,
And in this quirky rendezvous,
Every heart takes wing in flight.

## Puzzles Wrapped in Ribbon

A riddle wrapped in laughter's gown,
Twists the mind like pretzel dough,
Where every frown turns upside down,
And secrets dance like happy snow.

Jigsaw pieces sing in unison,
As ducks wear boots and ties to stroll,
Each clue is a silly mission,
Making sense of the whimsical whole.

Puzzles stacked with jokes inside,
Twist the path of every thought,
As giggles run away to hide,
In corners where confusion's caught.

So solve this maze of playful jest,
With ribbons that bind pure delight,
In a world where funny is the quest,
And laughter fills the endless night.

## Mirage of Mirth

A jester's hat, so bright and bold,
With riddles wrapped in tales untold.
Chasing shadows in a merry dance,
We stumble, giggle, and take a chance.

A pie in the sky, or is it here?
Splat! We're all covered in goo and cheer.
Mirth's elusive, like a wisp of smoke,
But laughter lingers with every poke.

A cat in a hat, a fish in a shoe,
The world spins round; what will we do?
With each misstep, we swirl and sway,
In this absurd game, we choose to play.

What's truth and what's just a funny truth?
In this circus, we're forever a sleuth.
Chasing giggles in an endless loop,
Join the madness, let's form a troupe.

## Lively Liaisons

Two friends in a kitchen, a recipe torn,
Eggs in the air, and the toast looks worn.
They giggle, they bumble, yet somehow succeed,
In crafting chaos, it's all that we need.

A parrot that talks in rhymes so strange,
With puns and jests, it's hard to arrange.
They laugh till they cry, in a tangle of chins,
In this whimsical world, who really wins?

Dates on the calendar, always a race,
We mix up the numbers; it's all out of place.
Yet through all the blunders, they shine and glow,
In this dance of the quirky, they steal the show.

With friends like these, the awkward's a prize,
In the game of mishaps, we win the surprise.
Embrace the blunders, let the good times flow,
Tomorrow we'll laugh at what we don't know.

## The Fable of Twisted Paths

Once in a land where the roads entwine,
A knotted old tree becomes quite divine.
With strange signposts that point to the moon,
We wander the paths humming a tune.

A squirrel in glasses studies a map,
While the rabbit declares, 'Let's take a nap!'
They argue and bicker, but giggles ensue,
In this land of oddities, what will they do?

The wanderers trip, then tumble with glee,
Grabbing at clouds, floating wild and free.
Each twist is a lesson, each stumble a gift,
In this fable of folly, we all get a lift.

As the stars align, they all finally see,
That the journey's the punchline, as bright as can be.
With a wink and a grin, they march on their quest,
For the joy of the ride trumps all of the rest.

## Conundrums of the Playful Spirit

In a world of questions, a riddle stands tall,
With playful spirits that dance in the hall.
They connect the dots in mismatched designs,
Solving square pegs in round, silly lines.

A toast to the mix-ups, the jests and the joy,
Where giggles burst forth like a child's favorite toy.
They spin on their heels, making castles of air,
In this breezy conundrum, they find everywhere.

A dog in a bowtie presides with a bark,
Chasing after wonders, igniting a spark.
In the whirl of confusion, they learn to embrace,
All the wild twists that they happily chase.

With humor as armor, they leap and they bound,
Crafting pure mischief while spinning around.
In the play of it all, they hear a faint cheer,
For the best of the moments are always quite near.

## The Humor Hidden in Shadows

In corners where giggles silently creep,
A jester slips when the watch is deep.
With shoes two sizes too big for his feet,
He dances in socks, oh what a treat!

The cat gives a glance, an eyebrow raised high,
As bread falls buttered — oh my, oh my!
A duck waddles by with a curious flap,
While someone trips over their own silly cap.

In shadows we find the quirkiest cheer,
A treasure of chuckles where no one can hear.
With each tiny slip as the night carries on,
The mischief is treasured as daylight is gone.

A flicker of joy in the slip of the light,
Where laughter takes flight and spins out of sight.
So gather your friends, let the giggles flow,
For moments like these are the best kind of show.

## Euphoria in the Unexpected

The toast pops up quick with a jump and a squeak,
As the cat makes a leap, oh the chaos this week!
A box of confetti spills out on the floor,
While an oven timer goes off like a roar.

A puddle of juice and a slip in the hall,
We sail through the kitchen, oh look at us fall!
With giggles contagious as laughter erupts,
A party of mishaps, our spirits are pumped.

The dog steals a donut and sprints with delight,
While we chase him around till we're breathless with fright.
Each twist in our tale brings a smile we can't hide,
In the whirl of the weird, there's a joy we abide.

So raise up a glass to the unexpected thrills,
To the moments of mayhem that fit like sweet frills.
For happiness dances where surprises abound,
In the heart of the silly, true joy can be found.

# **A Tapestry of Tickle and Twist**

In a world woven tight with stitches of fun,
A thread dangles loose where the laughter's begun.
Spools of mishaps, decisions gone wild,
Unravel our worries like a giggling child.

A banana peel tossed with a wink and a grin,
As someone skids past with a slip and a spin.
With squeals of delight as we tumble and roll,
Every hiccup is magic, it warms up the soul.

Puppies in pajamas are stealing the show,
As uncles breakdance, oh why do they glow?
A mix of pure whimsy in each tiny twist,
We gather together, the moments can't be missed.

So join in the weaving of giggles and play,
With patterns of cheer that brighten the day.
A tapestry stitched from the threads of our smiles,
Woven together, oh what fun for miles!

## Serenity in a Sea of Surprise

A calm breeze whispers through branches above,
While squirrels chime in like a chorus of love.
A picnic laid out, but the ants have arrived,
With twitching and squirming, our bounty is deprived.

A kite flies away with a colorful swoop,
As we chase the tail of a giggling group.
In a field of tall grasses, we tumble around,
With the echo of laughter, pure joy can be found.

A splash in the pond, oh what a delight!
As ducks in formation take off in their flight.
With water all soaked, and smiles ever wide,
We dance in the drizzle where silliness abides.

So let's raise our voices to moments so bright,
Where surprises unfold, and our hearts take flight.
With serenity wrapped in the chaos we make,
Each giggle, each snicker — our happiness stake.

## Meets and Mishaps

I tripped on a shoe,
That wasn't even mine,
Landed in a puddle,
Thought I'd be just fine.

A squirrel stole my snack,
Ran up a tree with glee,
I chased it in a fit,
Who's chasing who? Not me!

A phone call went amiss,
Talking to a bot,
I laughed 'til I cried,
What a strange thought!

But in this silly mess,
I find a spark of fun,
All these little quirks,
Make the day a run.

## The Roar of Quiet Giggles

In a room full of whispers,
A sneeze broke the calm,
A symphony of chuckles,
Like a soft, warm balm.

Chairs squeaked like they're laughing,
As folks told their tales,
Mismatched mugs, spilled cider,
How laughter never fails.

A cat jumped on the table,
With a graceful plop,
Knocked over our snacks,
We couldn't help but stop.

In the middle of the chaos,
We found our hidden cheer,
In the roar of quiet giggles,
Our hearts, bright and clear.

## **The Palette of Unplanned Joy**

Sunshine spilled like paint,
On cobblestone so bright,
I danced through the puddles,
In the clear morning light.

A bird decided to join,
Singing off-key so loud,
We laughed at the silly tune,
As it hopped in a crowd.

At the corner, a kid fell,
Landed right on some grass,
He giggled and jumped up,
Guess he'd planned out his class!

Every twist and turn,
Colors splashed in the air,
In this canvas of moments,
There's beauty everywhere.

## Topsy-Turvy Tales

There once was a cat,
Who thought it was a dog,
Chasing after the mailman,
Until he met a fog.

A goat in a sweater,
Trotted into a dance,
We questioned the fashion,
Should we give it a chance?

A cow tried to moo,
But it croaked like a frog,
We all stopped to wonder,
What's next in this fog?

In a world full of twists,
Where the silly takes flight,
Tales spin and unravel,
Under the moonlight.

# Hiccups in the Dance of Days

In the rhythm of morning haze,
A sock finds a friend, in the wildest ways.
Coffee spills like secrets untold,
While the cat plays king, oh so bold.

The sun beams rays, but the clouds play tricks,
As I trip on my thoughts, tangled in mix.
A dance on the edge, where giggles collide,
Here's to the whimsy, let chaos abide.

Chasing shadows that wink and sway,
In the corner of eyes, they wiggle and play.
With a skip and a hop, we twirl through the mess,
Finding joy in the fault, just brush off the stress.

So here's to the moments, a jumbled spree,
Where blunders are many, but hearts fly free.
In the hiccups of dance, let us sway and delight,
For every odd turn, we're stitched up tight.

## The Mischievous Melody

A tune that stumbles across the room,
With notes that giggle, dispelling the gloom.
The cat serenades with a purr and a leap,
As I fumble my steps, tiptoe, not creep.

The clock tick-tocks out of sync with a grin,
While I whistle a tune like I'm tuning a fin.
My keys take a trip to the fridge for a snack,
As laughter erupts from my voice, what a knack!

A spoon starts to dance with a fork in the fray,
Creating a song where the dishes all play.
With effort so light, we glide through the air,
In this kooky ensemble, nothing to compare.

So let us embrace this delightful charade,
Where singing and slipping in laughter is made.
In the mischief of sound, let joy find its tune,
As we waltz through the moments beneath the same moon.

## Enchanted by the Serendipitous Saga

Once upon a clumsy, silly spree,
A goat wore my hat—what a sight to see!
With a little bit of magic, I danced with a tree,
Whispered tales of wonder, wild and free.

The stars all giggled, twinkling with zest,
As I chased down my thoughts, the silliest quest.
A cookie defied gravity, soared through the night,
While I tried to catch dreams that took off in flight.

In the jumble of stories, and laughter unbound,
A chorus of quirks is where joy can be found.
With freckled delight, and a skip in my heart,
Each twist in the tale is a quirky sweet art.

Let's weave tales together, a tapestry bright,
Where mishaps and wonders help color the night.
In this enchanted moment, let chuckles take wing,
For in every enchantment, new joys we will bring.

## The Tickle of the Unforeseen

A shadow bumbled past with a wink and a nod,
As I tried to keep straight, but tripped and then trod.
A slip of the tongue turned into a jest,
Every flubbed little moment put humor to test.

The puddles called out for a hop and a splash,
With a grin and a giggle, I leaped with a dash.
The sun peeked around, tickling the air,
While I wobbled and swayed, like I hadn't a care.

The whims of the universe twisted and twirled,
In a dance of the unexpected, my heart was unfurled.
With a chalky blue sky and a splash of sweet cheer,
Every twist was a joy, every giggle sincere.

So gather those ticks that bring grins to our face,
In the whirl of the odd, let's embrace every trace.
For the tickle of moments—so playful, so bright,
They guide us with laughter, a wonderful flight.

## Unexpected Revelations

In a world of silly plots,
Where corsets meet the office pots,
I tripped on words, oh what a sight,
Laughing shadows stole the night.

A squirrel danced upon my head,
In meetings, whispers always spread,
Unexpected truths in crazy schemes,
Tickling hearts with wildest dreams.

At dawn, I found a rubber shoe,
Its partner lost, what could I do?
I wore it proudly down the street,
With each strange turn, life feels complete.

And every thought, a giggling sprite,
Confessions shared by candlelight,
As confusion reigns, I take a stand,
And revel in this wacky land.

## **Raucous Revelry.**

A party hat atop my hat,
With no clue where my cat is at,
Balloons that float beneath the moon,
Bring forth a wild and jolly tune.

The punch bowl spills, a colorful splash,
With every sip, I start to clash,
My dance moves great, yet quite absurd,
As laughter flows, the night's unheard.

Confetti rains from all around,
It's chaos in this festive ground,
And while we fumble, we still cheer,
For every blunder brings us near.

So raise a glass to all the weird,
To happy tears that once were feared,
In this mad whirl of joy and cheer,
Let's dance till morning's light is here.

## Whispers of a Playful Heart

In twilight's glow, I hear the tease,
Of giggling winds that dance with trees,
A heart that skips through paths unknown,
In whispered tales, I find my home.

Around the corner, laughter weaves,
While mischief hides beneath the leaves,
A playful breeze, a twist of fate,
Invites me onward, I can't be late.

With every step, a silly prank,
A hidden joke, a playful prank,
Where smiles bubble in vibrant hues,
And joy like buttercups renews.

So join the jest in nature's game,
Where every heart can find its fame,
In moments shared, we find the spark,
The magic glows in every park.

## The Jester's Embrace

A jester juggles thoughts anew,
With every laugh, a twist of view,
In motley gear, he takes his chance,
To lead the crowd in wobbly dance.

With painted smile, he spins around,
Creating joy where none is found,
His cap and bells a comedic sound,
Unraveling threads of thought unbound.

Through tangled words and crazy glee,
He weaves a tale just for thee,
Embracing quirks, the odd, the rare,
In this funhouse, none must care.

So let him laugh, and let him jest,
For every heart deserves a rest,
In humor's arms, we find our place,
Together lost in jester's grace.

## **Dizzy Days and Starry Nights**

The sun slips slow in painted skies,
As giggles meet the starry sighs,
A twist of fate, a caper grand,
Our tongues do tangle, but it's planned.

In dizzy days, we laugh till sore,
With every turn, we crave for more,
The night unfolds a sparkly tale,
Where nightly dreams set sail with gale.

With teddy bears in full balloon,
We dance like leaves in playful tune,
Confusion reigns, yet hearts collide,
In every stumble, love's the guide.

So raise a glass to night's delight,
To every star that feels just right,
In joyous chaos, we unite,
For life's a jest, a wild flight.

## Revelry in the Unanticipated

Unexpected giggles in the rain,
Silly dances, joy uncontained,
Umbrellas flip-flop, hats take flight,
With every splash, our hearts feel light.

Whispers of pranks behind closed doors,
Ticklish secrets, laughter pours,
A jester's grin, a grand parade,
In the confusion, the fun won't fade.

Banana peels on the kitchen floor,
As the cat leaps, we can't ignore,
Jokes on the tip of our wandering tongues,
Life's little quirks keep us young.

In mishaps, we find a dance,
Embracing blunders, taking a chance,
So let's toast to the whims and fates,
For joy finds us in laughing states.

## The Pilgrimage of Peculiar Joy

On winding paths of ups and downs,
We skip and hop, like playful clowns,
Oddball moments, like socks askew,
Each stumble leads to something new.

With mismatched shoes, we march ahead,
Chasing giggles, we laugh instead,
A mishap here, a blunder there,
In every folly, we find flair.

Tea spills, the cat gives a chase,
The kitchen's a hodgepodge of grace,
In spilled flour, we create art,
With messy hands and joyful heart.

Through tangled leaves and laughter loud,
We embrace the weird, we are proud,
Each twist, a badge of our delight,
On our pilgrimage of funny sights.

**Rhapsody of the Unseen**

A symphony played on clattering plates,
Spoons trumpeting at dinner dates,
Whiskers twitching with feline grace,
In the chaos, we find our place.

Marbles rolling, hiding under chairs,
Lost in giggles, we cast off cares,
A simple smile ignites the air,
In the unnoticed, joy is rare.

The clock strikes three, a dance ensues,
With socks on hands, we create the blues,
As wild confessions flow like wine,
We toast to moments, yours and mine.

Through blunders made and jokes retold,
In the unseen, we strike gold,
With open hearts, we tune our ears,
To the rhapsody of laughter's cheers.

## A Sparkle in the Ordinary

Beneath the mundane, a secret glows,
In coffee spills, our humor grows,
Toasters pop, with crumbs in flight,
Even mishaps taste just right.

Hiccups shared over morning bread,
With each silly quip, the worries shed,
Chortles echoed in cozy rooms,
Where joy unfurls and confusion blooms.

A mismatch found in vibrant socks,
As laughter bursts, the spirit unlocks,
In simple quirks, a spark ignites,
In the ordinary, the magic bites.

So let us revel in each small chance,
Embracing twirls in our daily dance,
For in the ordinary's embrace,
We find the spark, we find our place.

## The Cartwheel of Realities

In a world that's upside down,
We flip and spin, we wear a frown.
Yet joy is found in every blunder,
As giggles burst like summer thunder.

Chasing shadows that dance and sway,
Tripping over what people say.
The mysteries wrapped in a silly bow,
Make us question what we know.

With every twist and turn we take,
A giggle slips, a sneeze, a shake.
Round we go, a merry chase,
Finding humor in every place.

So cartwheel through this wacky scheme,
Laughter blooms, a bright daydream.
In chaos, there's a truth unspun,
That a little fun is never done.

## A Canvas of Peculiar Pleasantries

Brush strokes of joy in splatters wide,
Every color's got a story to confide.
With strokes so bold the shades collide,
Creating smiles we cannot hide.

A splash of blue, a dash of red,
Each brush with fate is never dread.
We paint our thoughts, both wild and shy,
Art becomes a sweet goodbye.

In this gallery of oddity,
Where even chaos finds its comedy.
Every canvas tells a tale,
Of laughter ringing like a bell.

So mix and mingle, grab a hue,
Create a masterpiece, that's all you do.
In peculiar tastes, we find our place,
A joyful heart, an artful grace.

## The Jumble of Jollity

A jumble sale of glee and cheer,
Where socks miss mates and hats draw near.
Laughter echoes in aisles of fun,
Mixed-up treasures for everyone.

Who knew a spoon could dance so well?
Or a teacup sing like a happy bell?
Amidst the chaos, giggles arise,
An orchestra of silly surprise.

Tangled in whims that lead astray,
But what's the point of knowing the way?
For every twist is a chance to play,
In this wobbly game, we're here to stay.

So grab a friend, let's sort this heap,
Unraveling laughter, a treasure to keep.
In every jumble, find the shine,
A perfect puzzle by design.

## The Sweet Serenade of Simple Surprises


Whispers of joy float through the air,
With butterflies dancing everywhere.
A sudden giggle at a fleeting glance,
Turns the mundane into a prancing dance.

Like socks that strut in mismatched pairs,
Or pies that end up in strange affairs.
Unexpected moments play and tease,
In this gentle breeze, we find our ease.

An accidental trip, a funny fall,
Turns solemn times into a rollicking call.
The serenade of quirks unfolds,
In sweet stories, life never grows old.

So let the melody of joy resound,
In every heart, let laughter abound.
For in the simplest things we find,
A wondrous tale that's one of a kind.

## Curves of Whimsical Wonder

In a world where socks go missing,
The cat curls up, a quiet king.
Chasing shadows on the wall,
We trip and laugh, and often fall.

A garden filled with jelly beans,
Where flowers wear their brightest greens.
The sun plays peekaboo with clouds,
And giggles dance in cheerful crowds.

We ride the waves of silly glee,
Balancing on a wobbly tree.
With every twist and turn we take,
A sprinkle here, a laugh to make.

So grab a friend and jump right in,
Embrace the chaos, let's begin!
For in this maze of quirk and cheer,
What's simple often feels quite dear.

## Trails of Playful Intrigue

In a maze of mismatched shoes,
We chase the paths that we can't choose.
Tickled by the winds that blow,
We giggle at the clumsy show.

A sprinkle of spice on vanilla ice,
Polliwogs dance, oh what a slice!
A turtle in a racing hat,
He puffs and ponders, 'How about that?'

With maps that lead us round and round,
To nowhere which is quite profound.
We leap through puddles, shriek with glee,
As ducks perform a ballet spree.

Each twist a riddle, every turn,
Laughter bubble, watch it churn.
In this grand chase of silly bliss,
We find the treasure that we miss.

## The Circle of Quicksilver Moments

Clockwatchers wring their hands so tight,
While rubber chickens take to flight.
A jester paints the town in stars,
And laughter echoes, near and far.

With juggling balls that never drop,
A pogo stick, we laugh and hop.
In bustling streets where whispers play,
We ride the wave of the silly sway.

While time unravels in its game,
Each fleeting tick, a spark of flame.
In every giggle, we reclaim,
The sparkle bright, the moment's name.

So swirl around in this soft glow,
Where joy's the path, we'll freely flow.
In circles wide, we skip and sing,
To quicksilver moments, joy we bring.

## The Frothy Brew of Existence

In morning cups where dreams are stirred,
A frothy swirl of thought is stirred.
Sugar sprinkles and giggles blend,
In every sip, a brand-new trend.

The toaster pops with a joyful tune,
While pancake stacks grow tall as noon.
Syrup rivers run wild and free,
As we flip pancakes with glee.

A game of hide and seek ensues,
With crayons and chairs and lots of cues.
Every corner hides a surprise,
As we peek through bright, laughing eyes.

So raise a glass to this delight,
Where chaos mixes with the light.
In this frothy brew, life's a tease,
In sips so sweet, we find our ease.

www.ingramcontent.com/pod-product-compliance
Lightning Source LLC
Chambersburg PA
CBHW051631160426
43209CB00004B/600